Cuando Sea Grande / When I Grow Up

PUEDO SER UNA CANTANTE/ I CAN BE A SINGER

By Alex Appleby   Traducido por Eida de la Vega

Gareth Stevens
PUBLISHING

Please visit our website, www.garethstevens.com. For a free color catalog of all our high-quality books, call toll free 1-800-542-2595 or fax 1-877-542-2596.

Library of Congress Cataloging-in-Publication Data

Appleby, Alex.
I can be a singer = Puedo ser una cantante / by Alex Appleby, translated by Eida de la Vega.
p. cm. — (When I grow up = Cuando sea grande)
Parallel title: Cuando sea grande
In English and Spanish.
Includes index.
ISBN 978-1-4824-0865-2 (library binding)
1. Singers — Juvenile literature. 2. Singing — Juvenile literature. 3. Occupations — Juvenile literature. I. Appleby, Alex. II. Title.
ML3930.A2 A66 2015
784—d23

First Edition

Published in 2015 by
Gareth Stevens Publishing
111 East 14th Street, Suite 349
New York, NY 10003

Editor: Ryan Nagelhout
Designer: Sarah Liddell
Spanish Translation: Eida de la Vega

Photo credits: Cover, p. 1 (singer) paulaphoto/Shutterstock.com; cover, p. 1 (stage) alphaspirit/Shutterstock.com; p. 5 Donald P Oehman/Shutterstock.com; p. 7 Sergey Novikov/Shutterstock.com; p. 9 Adam Taylor/Digital Vision/Thinkstock.com; p. 11 Antonio_Diaz/iStock/Thinkstock.com; p. 13 JGI/Jamie Grill/Blend Images/Getty Images; p. 15 Digital Vision/Digital Vision/Thinkstock.com; pp. 17, 24 (teacher) Christopher Futcher/Vetta/Getty Images; pp. 19, 23, Ned Frisk/Blend Images/Thinkstock.com; pp. 21, 24 (drums) Ned Frisk/Blend Images/Getty Images.

Printed in the United States of America

CPSIA compliance information: Batch #CS15GS: For further information contact Gareth Stevens, New York, New York at 1-800-542-2595.

Contenido

- -

Contents

Me gusta cantar.

I love to sing.

5

Tengo muy buena voz.

I have a great voice.

Cuando sea grande
quiero ser cantante.

I want to be a singer
when I grow up.

Me sé muchas canciones.

I know a lot of songs.

Me gusta cantar
en la escuela.

I like to sing at school.

Tomo muchas
clases de música.

I take many
music classes.

Tengo una
buena maestra.
Es una profesora
de canto.

I have a great teacher.
She is called
a voice coach.

Canto con mis amigos.

I sing with my friends.

Mi amiga Jane
toca la batería.

My friend Jane
plays the drums.

21

¡Tenemos una banda!

We have a band!

Palabras que debes saber/
Words to Know

(la) batería/
drums

(la) maestra/
teacher

Índice/Index